WORDS OF LIFE AND ENCOURAGEMENT

TRACY COOPER

Words Of Life And Encouragement

By Tracy Cooper

Cover Created by Jazzy Kitty Publications

Logo Designs by Andre M. Saunders/Leroy Grayson

Editor: Anelda L. Attaway

© 2022 Tracy Cooper 04/1/2022

ISBN 978-1-954425-37-8

Library of Congress Control Number: 2021923359

ACKNOWLEDGMENTS

God the Father, whom all blessings flow. He gave me my gift to share.

Also, Pastors Robyn and Marilyn Gool (Victory Christian Center- Charlotte, North Carolina)

To Brian Madeira and Dr. Sidney Jacobs, as well as Lilly McClinton and Cynthia Slater.

DEDICATIONS

This book is dedicated to Poinsettia Octoria Cooper, the greatest person I ever loved. You always encouraged me. You are surely missed; the world was blessed when you were around.

TABLE OF CONTENTS

TABLE OF CONTENTS

TABLE OF CONTENTS

INTRODUCTION

Words Of Life And Encouragement is a book of poetry and prose. A publication that is meant to engage and inspire the reader. It will serve as a message of hope.

They will be edified and enlightened. They will be able to identify with what they take in. The words will be on point, resonating with their souls edified.

INVITATION

EACH DAY I LIVE

I NEED YOU

TO HAVE YOUR WAY WITH ME

THE MARK I DON'T

WANT TO MISS

TAKE CONTROL THAT I'D BE

FREE

I TAKE MY HANDS OFF

Don't want to be Lost

Totally caught up in a World of Sin

Into my Heart

I fully let You in

To Blot Out all that Darkness

All the Iniquity

That has accumulated

Please take Control

Let this Soul be Illuminated

As I draw Near

To You

Draw Near to me

I have Suffered Long enough

Without You Deliver me

I Repent, Let Your Spirit

Fall afresh Upon me

I need You

Want You

I Desire to be

In Your Will, have Your way

I am Your child

Please Forgive

Those Transgressions

Which kept me

From You

I wanna be better

Hear Oh Lord My Plea

To my life You are

The Vital Crucial Key

Apart from You

I can do Nothing

Make something

Out of my Existence

I won't be No Longer

Resistant

I TAKE MY HANDS OFF

I TAKE MY HANDS OFF

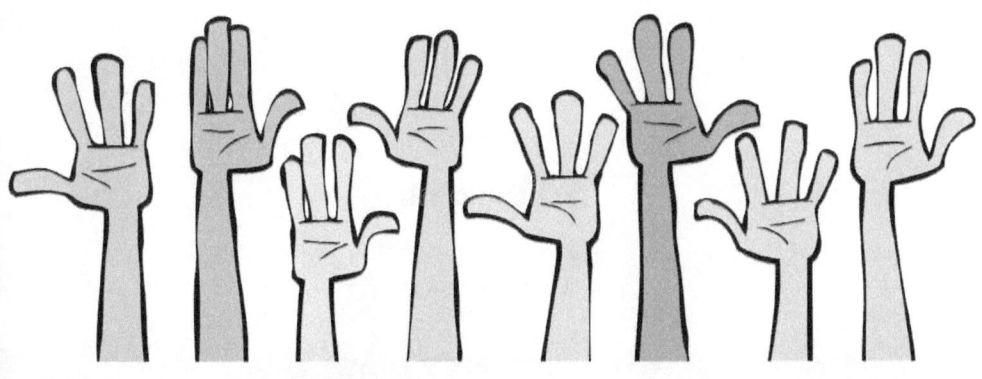

MAKE SOMETHING

OUT OF MY EXISTENCE

I WON'T BE NO LONGER

RESISTANT

I TAKE MY HANDS OFF

PURIFY YOUR HEART

So many think

I've gotten this Far

Without God

But you Woke up

By His Mercy new

And His Grace, that's enough

It's Poured upon

Even if you don't

Believe in Him

You are His

He is the Author and Finisher

Of your Story

Any Achievement

That you have Attained

You have not reached

That Milestone

On your own

But if you Fail

To Acknowledge Him

In your Life

He will let you Follow

The Wayward Way

You will have to Answer

What will you have to say

You think it is Good

Without Him

But really, you are Nothing

Without God

Everything

You have Attained

Will be Dead and Gone

Make Jesus

The Lord of your Life

Turn Away from Iniquity

PURIFY YOUR HEART

PURIFY YOUR HEART

MAKE JESUS

THE LORD OF YOUR LIFE

TURN AWAY FROM INIQUITY

PURIFY YOUR HEART

JUST LOVE

Love as much as you can

For God Loved you First

Love each other

Amen

Love

For God is Love

Love a Stranger

Love a Friend

Love your Family

Love is Required Each Day

Be Inspired to Love

Cause the World Needs Love

Always Give yours Away

JUST LOVE

JUST LOVE

BE INSPIRED TO LOVE

CAUSE THE WORLD NEEDS LOVE

ALWAYS GIVE YOURS AWAY

JUST LOVE

THERE IS NO TIME

There is No Time Like the Present

To get Right with God

Time is too Precious of a Commodity

Not to be aware

It moves Swiftly, waiting for no one

Redeem the time

Occupying every moment, Endeavoring to be Holy

Do not Waste your Time

I am talking to myself as well as you

This day Choose the Lord

While there Still is Time

Seize the Opportunity as you view this Evil Day

The adversary is seeking to Destroy and Devour

Whom he may

The Lord Thy God Obey

We can't afford to Hesitate in this Present Day

The Lord Jesus is coming Back any day

It could very well be Today

Are you ready to Fly Away

Disappear into Glory

Let God finish your story Favorably

So you have that Future and Hope

A Blessed Destiny

For Heaven, He has Prepared for us...

He is ready to Extend to us

This is His Plan and Expected End for us

To be with Him

To Study War No More

We must Endure

Because Time is Accelerating

In this Wicked Atmosphere

These are the Last Days

Change your Ways

BEFORE THERE IS NO TIME

THERE IS NO TIME

THESE ARE THE LAST DAYS

CHANGE YOUR WAYS

BEFORE THERE IS NO TIME

THE CRAZY STUFF GOING ON IN THE WORLD TODAY

Occurring daily everywhere

In emboldened ways

We must always be aware

To God, we must Pray

For so many Don't Care

About the way they Carry On

They behave so Terribly

Thinking they have done Nothing so bad

They call what is right Wrong

They call what is wrong Right

We need God to Intervene

To come In Between

Those who Perpetrate such Heinous Acts

And their Victims

Those in Authority need to Step Up

If they aren't Corrupt

And part of the problem

Justice must be Won

But don't look to man

To God cast your Cares

In regard to all of this

Because those who Dare

On Wrongdoing are fixed

For their Misdeeds, they will Pay

But Pray I say to you

Don't Wait Another Day

Not Another Moment

It's an Urgent Matter

That requires your Participation

Do your part

Pray about

THE CRAZY STUFF GOING ON IN THE

WORLD TODAY

THE CRAZY STUFF GOING ON IN THE

WORLD TODAY

DO YOUR PART

PRAY ABOUT

THE CRAZY STUFF GOING ON IN THE

WORLD TODAY

I CALL YOUR NAME

I CALL YOUR NAME

When there's Sorrow

And Pain

And endless Rain

On my Parade

I CALL YOUR NAME

As time is borrowed

We live it

Not in Vain

No Charade

I CALL YOUR NAME

When the Struggle

A Linked Chain

Won't Break

I CALL YOUR NAME

Despite

All my Troubles

For there's a Way of Escape

I CALL YOUR NAME

Believing

You are Faithful

And You will

Never Leave nor Forsake

I CALL YOUR NAME

Unashamed

Cause

I don't

Want to go

It alone

I CALL YOUR NAME

Because

Apart from You

I can do Nothing

On my own

I CALL YOUR NAME

For this Iniquity

And Sin

I must Atone

I CALL YOUR NAME

Because the Manifestation

Of Victory

Is with You

All Along

I CALL YOUR NAME

For all Your

Mercy and Grace

By Your Power

I am made Strong

Therefore

I Carry On

I CALL YOUR NAME

Cause

You are my Strong Tower

I run to You

And I am Safe

I am home

I CALL YOUR NAME

For You made a way

From No Way

I CALL YOUR NAME

For You are Love

I CALL YOUR NAME

I CALL YOUR NAME

I CALL YOUR NAME

WHEN THE STRUGGLE

A LINKED CHAIN

WON'T BREAK

LIFE IS A LONG SEASON

LIFE IS A LONG SEASON

But we must Redeem All of its Time

We must Endure any Punches

It has to throw

By going from Glory to Glory

Letting the ALMIGHTY

Be the Author and Finisher

Of your Story

Obtain Joy

Leap for it

Exercise Faith

Reach out to others

Tell them about Jesus

While you Embrace this Hope

And let them know

He is Enough

For every Challenge they Face

With determination, Run the Race

As each day

With Mercy and Grace

Receive

In God Believe

YES, LIFE IS A LONG SEASON

But Go with God

He is MORE than Enough

To get you Through

LIFE IS A LONG SEASON

OBTAIN JOY

LEAP FOR IT

EXERCISE FAITH

REACH OUT TO OTHERS

TELL THEM ABOUT JESUS

LIKELY STORY

You Can't Believe

Mostly anything

That you Hear

Oftentimes You must Read

Between the Lines

It's Unclear

It could be Factual or Fiction

Manufactured

It seems like mostly everyone

In a Cold and Wicked World

Is not Honest

If it's not Scamming or Duping

I suppose it's Pranking or Cheating

Catfishing

Pretending

Alter ego

Details deleting

Living vicariously

Through someone else

Prideful

Not asking for Help

When needed

Hiding

We all have done this

In one way or another

An out and out one

Or, by omission, it would come

Some don't ask for Forgiveness

By these, so many suffer

Many think they are getting away

But by and by

They will be found out

For their Version of Truth

They'll have to Pay

They will have to Answer

For Make Believe

A Non-Absolute

Fabrication

A False Tale

Infamous Glory

LIKELY STORY

LIKELY STORY

YOU CAN'T BELIEVE

MOSTLY ANYTHING

THAT YOU HEAR

OFTENTIMES YOU MUST READ

BETWEEN THE LINES

IT'S UNCLEAR

SO CLOSE

I heard of someone

Who fell Prey to Covid

Someone who knew someone

I knew

One of thousands Adding to Statistics

A Casualty of the Pandemic

But it wasn't on the news

It was somewhat in my Circle

All the while you think

Gone Too Soon

And yes, they were a Stranger

A third party

Nevertheless

A Life

Ravaged

And Ruined

By this Dreaded Disease

And you Wonder

Could their life

Have been Saved

Were there Measures in Place

Did they have to go to an Early Grave

Painful

SO CLOSE

SO CLOSE

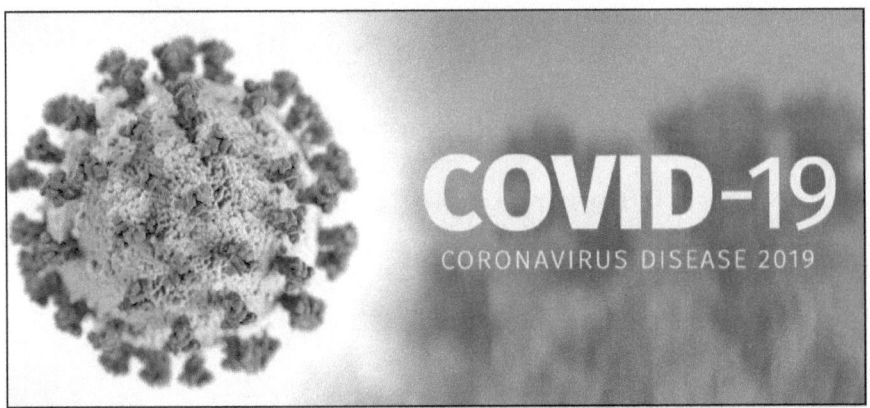

I HEARD OF SOMEONE

WHO FELL PREY TO COVID

SOMEONE WHO KNEW SOMEONE

I KNEW

ONE OF THOUSANDS ADDING TO

STATISTICS

A CASUALTY OF THE PANDEMIC

BUT IT WASN'T ON THE NEWS

LEAVE ME

Somebody told me I was Blessed

To have experienced Love

One time than Not At All

Nowadays,

When folks will up and go

Yes become Phased

Don't get their way

Unable to stick it out

Not making Allowance in any way

They don't give Love a Chance to Grow

Themselves are what they are all about

My bride and I were Nothing like these

So yes, I guess that individual was Right

Our Love was Special Indeed

I'm not saying we didn't Fight

We had Conflicts, but we Believed

We could work them out

So **LEAVE ME** to my Bittersweet Reality

That I remain so Lonely

Perhaps there is still a Possibility

That I will know Love Once More

But it seems a Remote Chance

Like slim and none

LEAVE ME

A FAMILY REUNION

I don't know what occurred

I never got to know

My Relatives

Kinfolk

My Family

I met some A few years back

At a Funeral

I have heard some things

But I don't know why we aren't close

But I desire to see them

And fellowship share

Sit down and Pleasantries Extend

Talk about Traditions

Visit with all the Generations

Love like a Family should

And say from my Lips

This is So Good

A FAMILY REUNION

A FAMILY REUNION

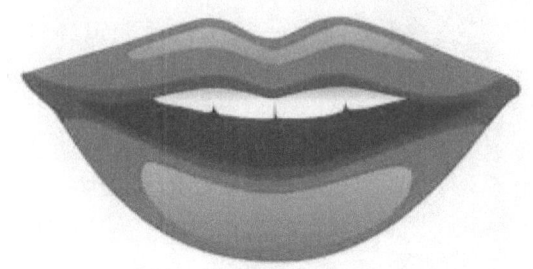

LOVE LIKE A FAMILY SHOULD

AND SAY FROM MY LIPS

THIS IS SO GOOD

A FAMILY REUNION

LIVES LOST

On the News

I heard the term Collective

In regard to the Number

OF LIVES LOST

And those to follow

I know they MUST Address it

Categorize it

But these **LIVES**

Deserve to be Dignified

Put some Respect upon their Name

For so many in multiple thousands

By this Scourge of Covid have Perished

Their Memory, even by the Lawmakers

Those who Hold Office should be Cherished

Let me say that this is not directed toward

Everyone in DC

But really. . .

We should not be Disrespectful

JUST ANOTHER PERSON

To be among the many

Disappearing in the Crowd

Not needlessly detained by any

Not for my Life Screaming Out Loud

Not being Paranoid

Constantly looking over my Shoulder

Of freedom being Void

The Oppression falling on me like Boulders

Just having as a person the Dignity that is Deserved

Being a Human Soul that God created

Not Paralyzed by Mistreatment

Nor Perturbed

But by Peace, so very Elated

So many who are Resembling me

That to me, have No Aversion

Not wanting to do any Harm to me

Absolutely Free

JUST ANOTHER PERSON

SPARKLE

Like a Diamond So Shine

Life's not Succumbing to Pressure

Being tough-minded to Endure

Enlightening the Darkness

Even though you may be Sore

SPARKLE In life's nighttime sky

A star always having Luster

Still maintaining composure

Ever so Radiant

SPARKLE with a beaming Smile

The Jewel God made so Precious

You have a Place in Society

You are so Relevant

SPARKLE with your uniqueness

Illuminate

You have Purpose and Promise

A true sure enough Destiny

A particular Brilliance

SPARKLE, realize you are fine

Be amazing because you are formed in God's Image

You are Very Special

Beautiful

SPARKLE

Oh So Shine

SPARKLE

LIKE A DIAMOND, SO SHINE

LIFE'S NOT SUCCUMBING TO PRESSURE

BEING TOUGH-MINDED TO ENDURE

ENLIGHTENING THE DARKNESS

EVEN THOUGH YOU MAY BE SORE

AVAILABLE

The task before me

Truly

Surely

Is not too Great

Because You can work with

With what I have

I am Furnished and Equipped

For every Good Work

In all my Imperfections

You Transform

YouTranslate

Without Doubt

I do not Hesitate

There is No Resistance

As I make myself

AVAILABLE to You

Oh God

WORRY WORT

From Day-to-Day

Things change

In an Accelerated Way

And you feel

You can't keep up

With the Pace

Because you weren't the same

As your Counterparts

So here you remain

In the world Apart

Trying to Save Face

In order to Survive

Limited opportunities

You trying to maintain

With a diminished Skillset

But DO NOT Fret

Your worth isn't Less

God will STILL Bless

You're Coming and Going

Put your Trust in Him

In order not to Regret

He knows what you stand in need of

If you put Him first

All these things will be added unto you

Do not become a **WORRY WORT**

SABBATH REST

Some say It's Sunset to Sunset

Friday to Saturday

Caught up in a Day

Hooked by a calendar

But I say

We are to come Away

And Have That Sacred Time

With Him

Anytime

Anyplace

In your Secret Closet

Being Intimate

With

The ALMIGHTY

Having Fellowship

With Good

Pursuing Him

In Holiness

To receive Instruction

And Insight

What A Delight

To come Away

With Him

On the

SABBATH REST

SABBATH REST

2021

January 2021	February 2021	March 2021	April 2021

May 2021	June 2021	July 2021	August 2021

September 2021	October 2021	November 2021	December 2021

SOME SAY IT'S SUNSET TO SUNSET

FRIDAY TO SATURDAY

CAUGHT UP IN A DAY

HOOKED BY A CALENDAR

BUT I SAY

WE ARE TO COME AWAY

BREAKING NEWS

We have a Bulletin

A Special Report

Pressing an Alert

BREAKING NEWS

It's Clear

Evidently, the Time is Near

Man's Coldness and Indifference

And Violence

And Disease

And Disaster

So many don't Believe it

They just won't Receive it

Heed it

They Refuse to Read it

The Signs

Which are in Place

They will not Embrace

THIS BREAKING NEWS

BREAKING NEWS

IT'S CLEAR

EVIDENTLY, THE TIME IS NEAR

WHAT CAN YOU BE SURE OF

Everything And Almost Everyone

Is a game

You must Figure Out

You will know them

By their Fruits

If it's low Hanging, Withering

Or if it has Completely

Taken Root Fully Ripened

It may be a Good Season

Or the Crop may be Ruined

What will you Choose

To be fully Certain

What kind of Scruples do they Possess

Are they Guided by the right Kind of Principles

Do they have the right Kind of Associations

Are they the right Kind of People

Over time their Fruit will show

WHAT CAN YOU BE SURE OF

GOD BE WITH YOU

Ever since I remember

We have Spoken it

Declaring it to be so

When we have Applied it

Safely on our Journey, We Would Go

A Measure of Faith that all this time

We have uttered Just Thinking

That God was So True

Gave such Assurance

Four words Spoken

Rang So True

In your Spirit

Solitude

These words

I heard

Served as a Catalyst

To each day, Guide me Through

That's why I still Speak them Today

GOD BE WITH YOU

SAY HELLO

What Does it Cost to Speak

In Passing or Sitting next to Somebody

It doesn't Mean

You are Weak

Or let your Guard Down

Unless you are not that Desirable

To be around

The Book of Life

The Bible

God's Love Letter

Says that those

Who show themselves

Friendly

Shall have Friends

And I know Everyone

That we come upon

That we Meet

May not be to our Liking

But we MUST Remember

That God is Love

And we

You and me

Are made in His Image

Spare Politeness

Let God's Love

Shine through You

As you could be making their day

SAY HELLO

THE BOOK OF LIFE

THE BIBLE

GOD'S LOVE LETTER

WHAT KIND OF LOVE IS THIS

Unparalleled

Remarkable

Steadfast

And

Unmovable

Day in and Day out, Forgiving

When we didn't deserve it

And Nothing Can Separate you

From it

Of course, we should not

In any way Sin

But our God is Plentiful

In Mercy

And each day

Blesses us

With Grace

What can you say about this

Reflection upon it

Can make you Speechless

Or just move you to Tears

Raise your Hands, Praising Him

Or Bow Down in Worship

Because you just know

Ain't nobody

Never gonna Care for you like this

Even after the Mark, you have Missed

Leaving you asking the Question

WHAT KIND OF LOVE IS THIS

ACCOUNTABILITY

None is Perfect, but Jesus

But that doesn't Dismiss us

We still must put in the Work

Gotta have the mind to be

Striving for Perfection

Holy and Acceptable

In His Eyesight become

When we are before Him

On the day

Will God say Well Done

My Good and Faithful Servant

What then will you say about it

Will you have a Case

You don't have to Justify

We can't afford to be Reckless

Every moment It's Precious

Cast aside every Weight

Before it is actually Too Late

Really. . . truly, we CAN NOT Wait

Make sure you are Careful

To perform the Great Commission

And treat everyone Right

Ask God for Insight

Be on a Mission

To be on One Accord

Just living Right

Being a Delight

So you can have **ACCOUNTABILITY**

KEEP LOOKING AT THE SKY

Keep looking up

Lift your head up

Maintain your View

Beyond the Clouds

Stay focused on GOD ALMIGHTY

Yes. . . NEVER lose Sight of

The abundance of His Manifold Blessings

His Everlasting Love

Thank God for this

Verbalize it

Your Voice in Exceedingly Joy

Give Him Praise

With your Hands Raised

KEEP LOOKING AT THE SKY

Keenly toward Heaven

A clear view

Knowing no matter what Challenges

You may face in this Earthly Realm

You must not become Down Casted

No NOT Overwhelmed

Because for you, He has a Future and a Hope

A Plan and Expected End

So when you Hear your Mind

Tell you that it's all in Vain

Listen to your Spirit

And your Focus Maintain

KEEP LOOKING AT THE SKY

For God is for you

And NOT against you

KEEP LOOKING AT THE SKY

KEEP LOOKING AT THE SKY

FOR GOD IS FOR YOU

AND NOT AGAINST YOU

KEEP LOOKING AT THE SKY

RELEASE ME

Lord Lay hold of me

As I seek You

Take me

From this Retched Place

Have Mercy

I want to go

From Glory to Glory

As I Endeavor to be on One Accord

Help me to Press Forward

To Savor Your Grace

I am not fixed

On Material Things

Your Praises I Sing

So, the Joyful Salvation You Bring

Exercising my Faith to come up Higher

To see a different result

Than that Prior

Please Forgive any Transgressions

That I may have against me

My intent is Repentance

So that I may be Transparent

That to me a Trajectory

Is apparent Father

I yield to do things

Your way Helps discipline me

No attention

To my Flesh Pay

In this way increase me

TELL SOMEONE

Let it be known the Reason for Hope

Make Somebody aware

Of the reason, you more than Cope

TELL SOMEONE about Jesus

And the Sacrifice He made

And the Everlasting Life He Gave

Upon a Cross at Calvary

TELL SOMEONE

To give their Heart to Jesus

Tell them

He Died for all their Sins

To Set them Free

If the Opportunity opens up

Don't keep it to yourself

It's Life-Changing

TELL SOMEONE

ABOUT JESUS

TELL SOMEONE

TELL SOMEONE ABOUT JESUS

AND THE SACRIFICE HE MADE

AND THE EVERLASTING LIFE HE GAVE

UPON A CROSS AT CALVARY

TELL SOMEONE

TO GIVE THEIR HEART TO JESUS

SAY IT RIGHT

Make right Confession

Speak well

Say what He says about you

Doing that What God Says to do

That which is so True

His Instruction is Full Proof

Part of it is Placing

It in the Atmosphere

So your Spirit receives

And your Soul Hears

It is Ammunition

That puts you in Position

To overcome

Having Victory

SO SAY IT RIGHT

HEARING

In your heart, Know the urging

Of the Spirit

Giving instruction

So you can Press On

To the Mark of the Higher Calling

Rarely audible

But you will recognize

You will realize Sense Deeply

Perceive Sweetly in your **HEARING**

FORGIVE

Every time what you think of someone

And you have a Tendency to Feel Badly

About them

You go back

And you don't let Bitterness Subside

There is a Fence you MUST Mend

Don't let it be your Guide

Past Hurt, DO NOT let it Thrive

In your Heart and Soul

Don't go there; Surrender your Pride

Or else it will Eat You Up Inside

Mentally and Physically

The Chance don't Deny

FORGIVE

GIVE YOU AWAY

Furnished and Equipped

For every Good Work

Invest in someone

Do good

There is a person

God has for you to Reach Out to

Perhaps an individual

You never met

A perfect pairing, So be of Service

Many need it

So go ahead and let them Receive it

GIVE AWAY YOU

FOLLOW

He doesn't have a

Social Media Page

Yet,

He does remain all the Rage

Angels and Humans sing His Praise

He has so many likes

By God's exploits, you would be Amazed

Beyond hype, He created you and I

Yeah, God Most High

El Shaddai

God of MORE than enough

And His Son

The Man The Very One

Who Saves Souls?

King of Kings

The Lord Jesus

His Name is ABOVE ALL THINGS

Now He is definitely someone

You should **FOLLOW**

FOLLOW

HE DOESN'T HAVE A

SOCIAL MEDIA PAGE

YET,

HE DOES REMAIN ALL THE RAGE

ELITE STREETS

In the Twentieth Century

In some cities in the South

In segregated sections

Black communities we're Bustling

Tulsa, Little Rock, and Durham

To name a few

They were enterprising

And dollars spent there

Recirculated several times

They were Thriving

On those **ELITE STREETS**

ELITE STREETS

BLACK COMMUNITIES WE'RE BUSTLING

TULSA, LITTLE ROCK, AND DURHAM

TO NAME A FEW

THEY WERE ENTERPRISING

AND DOLLARS SPENT THERE

GOING HOME

You Don't Drive a Fast Car

You Don't Play your Music Loud

You Don't Have Tinted Windows

You have Factory Wheels

You observe the Traffic Laws

Pretty unassuming

You are a Target anyway

Driving while Black or Brown

Headed to your House

Not too far away

Blue Lights in your Rear-View Mirror

They are Pursuing you

You haven't done anything Wrong

The officer exits his Vehicle

And approaching yours

He asks where I am coming from

I respond Work

You think that he is up to something

He asks if he can see my License

You reach to Retrieve it Slowly

I hand it to him

The officer goes back to his Cruiser

To run the License

He returns saying everything Checked Out

Saying a vehicle similar to yours was Stolen

Apologized for any inconvenience

This may have caused

Handing back my License

Got in his vehicle

And went on his way

That five minutes was Aggravating

To say the least

GOING HOME

Tracy Cooper

GOING HOME

THE OFFICER EXITS HIS VEHICLE

AND APPROACHING YOURS

HE ASKS WHERE I AM COMING FROM

I RESPOND WORK

GOD AS FATHER

Know Him Really

Truly Become Intimate

With

The ALMIGHTY

Better Acquainted

Connect With Him

Drawing Near In His Presence

To receive Instruction

Savoring His Essence

Not only In a Spiritual Reverential Way

But personally Knowing

GOD AS FATHER

ENOUGH

Made in the Image of God

The Father and Son

Endowed with the same Power

From on High

That raised Jesus from the Dead

Furnished and Equipped

For Every Good Work

Don't question or with inferiority

Identify If you are a Willing Vessel

You are indeed **ENOUGH**

STAY IN YOUR LANE

Just because You don't stand

In the Pulpit delivering the Word

Doesn't mean You are not a Minister

Right where you are

On your Job

In your Home

We are the Church

The only Representation

Of God, some may ever see

Yes, your Life they are Watching

Yes, through your particular Expertise

You are an Instrument

Don't covet after

What God didn't mean

For you to have

You have a certain Lay of the Land

To be that Light in a Dark World

Be Obedient

Shine

Reflect

STAY IN YOUR LANE

STAY IN YOUR LANE

RIGHT WHERE YOU ARE

ON YOUR JOB

IN YOUR HOME

WE ARE THE CHURCH

ELSEWHERE

Not just in the Building

Led by a Pastor

Or a Praise Team

Worship

Can be done

In-between

Sundays

You can always

Pray and Study

In your own time

Not just for One Day

Put in the Work

The time more than spare

With God spend Significant Time

A Lifestyle

Do the Work

Make the Sacrifice

On more than One Day

ELSEWHERE

MEAN THOUGHTS

Unsaid Yet unpleasant

Full of Malice, Tearing Down

Meditations NOT AT ALL Holy

Milling around in our Minds

Reservation We find

Prejudice with Our Hearts

Align

Sadly, these Words

Smarting off Silently

Making Judgment Vehemently

Totally unnecessary Eating away

Keeping mum on Ugly Words

Racist Discriminatory

Preconceived notions

From what has been handed down

Generations of Hatred and Dislike

Not needing to be Verbalized

Don't need to Thrive

Or Survive

Let them Subside

Forever

MEAN THOUGHTS

CHRISTMAS EVERY DAY

Goodwill to our Fellow Man

A feeling Comes over us

This time of year is Magical

People are more Apt to Reach Out

Love is Exchanged Freely

We remember Our Savior's Birth

The mood is so very Light, Momentarily

Ideally, We Behave Civilly

Why can't it be

CHRISTMAS EVERY DAY

CHRISTMAS EVERY DAY

LOVE IS EXCHANGED FREELY

WE REMEMBER OUR SAVIOR'S BIRTH

THE MOOD IS SO VERY LIGHT,

MOMENTARILY

IDEALLY, WE BEHAVE CIVILLY

WHY CAN'T IT BE

CHRISTMAS EVER YDAY

THINK BEFORE YOU SPEAK

You know how in your Flesh

You React and you Say

Something you Regret

That you cannot Take Back

You don't realize

But it's Second Nature

And you are ready to Pounce

You automatically have that Knack

I urge you to Stop

Before you act on Carnal Instincts

And another Soul Devours

You must Cut that person some Slack

So, before you have to Repent to God

And Apologize for how you have Behaved

Think before you Act

You must **THINK BEFORE YOU SPEAK**

WHY COMPLAIN

You may be in Dire Straits

And you may have succumbed

To a Lesser Fate

From the Routine, you have to Break

Perhaps you feel like no difference

You make

But I tell you, Resist the Urge

To be Fed Up or the Surge

That says Give Up

And the Blues just Shake

And from Lemons, Lemonade make

And now. . .even now

Be at Peace; On God, WAIT

Because it's not in Vain

Rejoice

Cause God is Working it Out

WHY COMPLAIN

WHY COMPLAIN

THAT SAYS GIVE UP

AND THE BLUES JUST SHAKE

AND FROM LEMONS, LEMONADE MAKE

TRANSPARENCY

Why Can't folks be Genuine

Forthright, Upfront, and Honest

Instead of Scamming

Trying to get over Catfishing

Why must they do this?

I much rather would carry on

When the Truth is expressed Liberally

Even when we may Disagree

TRANSPARENCY

GOOD GOD

He let us Rise

Tasting

His Sweet Grace

If we are in a Bind

We Can His Mercy Find

He makes a Way of Escape

Time after Time

Day after Day

We must be Thankful

For God Is Faithful

We are So Very Blessed

To have a **GOOD GOD**

LOVE IS SOMETHING YOU DO

To say it is One Thing

But to Act on it is completely Another

Someone let them your Love

Discover

You never know what someone

Is Going Through

But you Reaching Out

May be just what they Need

To Pull them Through

Make them aware

Of Compassion

Love isn't just SOMETHING you Say

LOVE IS SOMETHING YOU DO

HEART OF GOLD

One of the sweetest Human beings

To ever walk Upon the Earth

She was Regal, A Queen

But Humble

Civil with all people

She wanted folk to be Alright

She genuinely cared

About their Well Being

Worked at a Shelter

Told folks about Jesus

She had a Gentle Disposition

People spoke well of her being

One of the Great Ones

That we were Fortunate to be seeing

A Good Person

Totally Unselfish

Such a Beautiful Blessing

Rare. . . a Diamond

She is missed

Had a Glow Shining

Gone with God now

She was something

To behold

Having a **HEART OF GOLD**

SAY SOMETHING PRETTY

In this world Today

People Need to Hear

A Word of Encouragement

That it's Okay

Just like food

To their Spirit Nourishment

To keep them going

Speak Kind Words

Building someone up

Give Peace

Tell them who they are

In Christ Jesus

That they matter

And they're Precious

In His Sight

Mention they might want to Start

Living Right

All the while, to them, be a Light

Seasoning your Speech with Salt

Something they can Savor

A fullness Rich to which they can be Exposed

Causing Jubilation

SAY SOMETHING PRETTY

BE THANKFUL

Picking yourself up Off the Ground

Working hard to make it to this Point

It was by God's Grace you got here

You Excelled and Triumphed

By God placing you

In this Place of Power

You had the Favor of God

Upon your Life

You were Formed from Clay

Be ever so Humble

Because

In an instant

IT ALL COULD BE TAKEN AWAY

For apart from God, you can do Nothing

BUT CAN DO ALL THINGS IN CHRIST JESUS

Give God Glory

For being the Author and Finisher of your Story

Realize you did not One Thing on your own

Unless you got involved with the adversary

So up the Corporate Ladder, you were Carried

You think that you have Achieved this all Alone

God did it

He let you Make it

Don't act like you belong on a Pedestal

Be Humble

BE THANKFUL

HOOKED BY A FEELING

Happiness

Is a mere Phase

After feeding your Emotions

It never ever can stay

It's brief,

Momentary

However, Joy is a Knowing

Constantly Flowing

Having no shut off valve

With Joy be involved

Seek God all the Time

As you come to find

You have that Assurance

Blessed

Continuing

Confidence

A Confirmation

In your Heart and Mind Revealing

More than being

HOOKED BY A FEELING

SING OF HIS GOODNESS

He has done Great Things

Make it known

Lift your voice to Sing

Don't keep it to yourself

For God has NEVER Left Us Alone

When we Draw Near to Him

He will do the same for us

Each Day we Open our Eyes

It's by His Grace

We have more than Enough

His Mercy we once more Taste

When we find ourselves in Difficulty

He makes a Way of Escape

Not subjecting us to a Lesser Fate

So, Melody Make

Always

SING OF HIS GOODNESS

WE OUGHT TO PRAY

Cast our Cares

Is what we need to do

Each Day Turn from our Wicked way

And just be True

From Moment to Moment

When Someone or Something

Crosses our minds

Talk to God about it

Find the time

Just Pray

And don't ever Struggle

With Burdens

We were NEVER meant to Carry

Give them to God

And for Our Leaders

Ask God to be with them

And in Matters of Policy

Ask the Lord to Intervene

By Praying, We can have an Impact

On Society

Pray that captives would be Set Free

Pray for your Children and Marriage

PRAY EVERY DAY ALWAYS

The desires of your Heart

Simply because we need God to have His way

Will you Pray Today

WE OUGHT TO PRAY

WE OUGHT TO PRAY

THE DESIRES OF YOUR HEART

SIMPLY BECAUSE WE NEED GOD TO

HAVE HIS WAY

WILL YOU PRAY TODAY

WE OUGHT TO PRAY

STAY FREE

Don't put on Anything

That is Troubling, Meddling, Menacing

Let it Go

Don't get Tangled Up in a Web of Strife

Don't let the enemy

Whisper in your Ear

Lies you don't want to Hear

Put him in his place

Rebuke him

Place him under your Feet

In the Name of Jesus

Refuse to Comply

Remind him that his time is short

Not believing his Report

God is Sovereign

In Your Life

STAY FREE

WORDS

Spoken Softly, they Comfort

Heal and put at Ease

Like shade beneath a Cooling Tree

Laying upon your Soul Pleasantly

A Uttered ever so Gently

Soothing sweetly your Soul

Making you feel a certain way

Completely Full and Whole

Quiet words playing a Definite Role

Stroking your Psyche

You become Highly Likely

In turn towards others

To be so very kind

Tone of the voice Monotone

You are a participant in a Friendlier Zone

A subdued atmosphere

A Lovely Person does now appear

You now desire to Build-up

And not so terribly Tear Down

Low Key, you partake of Joy's Cup

Communication can be Jubilation

Full of positive Feedback and Elation

One can connect having a Calming Effect

When they come Correct with their WORDS

IF I COULD LOVE SOMEONE

IF I COULD LOVE SOMEONE

Share My Heart

Then I would not become

Left in this Dark Place

Much Maligned

Instead, I would have

So much Spark

Not a minimal Trace

Enlightening My Soul

Devoted, Expressing, Affection

And Care

Working toward that End

Being A Husband

A Faithful Friend

Kind, Understanding

Treasure, Soulmate

IF I COULD LOVE SOMEONE

ABOUT THE AUTHOR

INTRODUCING TRACY COOPER

Tracy Cooper Is a graduate of the University of Delaware. He developed an affinity for writing poetry from the age of 12, which has lasted until this very day.

Tracy has written several books of poetry, including:

- Seas Sands Poems Pictures 2012,
- Grace And Mercy 2019 (liberation publishing)...
- Pray Don't Faint. . . Believe (2021)

Words Of Life And Encouragement is his fourth book which is available worldwide.

REFERENCES FOR THE IMAGES

The following pictures were retrieved for the internet

1.Banner

2.bigstock-Read-Between-the-Lines-road-si-75611284

3.965380-breaking-news-ap-telangana-india

4.Calendars-With-Holidays

5.cartoon-hands-26782004

6.1381992377000-policeford

7.DOLLARS

8.europe-globe

9.heart-3d-model-sldprt-sldasm-slddrw

10. gettyimages-101286817-640x640

11. HTB1KYWbrSYTBKNjSZKbq6xJ8pXag

12. IMG_20140625_110805_148

13. istockphoto-155137713-170667a

14. KVwAPYK

15. LEAP

16. LIPS

17. love-angle_23989521711_o-X2-1024x686

18. merry-christmas-wish-christmas-tree-in-snow

19. money-Medium

20. prayer

21. SKY

22. social_media

23. SCALETHEBIBLE

24. wp3854497